C000180471

Greenland

Moira Buffini's plays include *Welcome to Thebes* (2010) at the National Theatre; *A Vampire Story* (2008), an NT New Connections play; *Dinner* (2002) at the NT and Wyndham's; *Loveplay* (2001) for the RSC at the Pit; *Silence* (1999), commissioned by the NT Studio and performed at Birmingham Rep and Plymouth Theatre Royal, winner of the Susan Smith Blackburn Prize; *Gabriel* (1997) at the Soho Theatre, winner of LWT Plays on Stage Award and Meyer Whitworth Award; and *Blavatsky's Tower* (1997) for the Machine Room. Adaptations include *Dying For It* from Nikolai Erdman's *The Suicide*, and *Marianne Dreams* from Catherine Storr's book, both for the Almeida (2007). Screenplays include *Tamara Drewe* directed by Stephen Frears (2010) and *Jane Eyre* directed by Cary Fukunaga (2011), both for Ruby Films, and an adaptation of *A Vampire Story* for Number 9 Films.

Matt Charman's plays include *The Observer*, *The Five Wives of Maurice Pinder* (both at the National) and *A Night at the Dogs* (at Soho Theatre), which won the Verity Bargate Award for new writers. He was previously Pearson Writer in Residence at the National and was recipient of the Peggy Ramsay Award. *The Observer* won the 2008 Catherine Johnson Award for Best Play, as part of the Pearson Playwrights' Scheme.

Penelope Skinner has been part of the Royal Court Young Writers Programme and Future Perfect with Paines Plough. Her plays include *Eigengrau* (Bush) and *Fucked* (Old Red Lion and Assembly Rooms, Edinburgh). Radio includes *The Old Road*, a *Man in Black* mystery (BBC Radio 7).

Jack Thorne's plays include *Bunny* (Nabokov, Fringe First Award), *2nd May 1997* (Bush Theatre/Nabokov), *Burying Your Brother in the Pavement* (NT Connections), *Two Cigarettes* (Bush Theatre), *Stacy* (Tron, Arcola Theatre and Trafalgar Studios), *Fanny and Faggot* (Pleasance Edinburgh, Finborough and Trafalgar Studios), *When You Cure Me* (Bush), *Paperhouse* (Flight 5065) and *Solids* (Paines Plough/Wild Lunch at the Young Vic). TV includes *This Is England 86* (with Shane Meadows), *The Fades*, *Cast-Offs* (with Tony Roche and Alex Bulmer) and episodes of *Skins* and *Shameless*. Films include *The Scouting Book for Boys*, which premiered at the 2010 London Film Festival, for which he won the Best British Newcomer Award. Radio includes *People Snogging in Public Places* (Winner of Best Drama at the Sony Radio Academy Awards 2010), *The Hunchback of Notre Dame* (Winner of the Radio Award at Ability Media International Awards 2009), *Left at the Angel* and *When You Cure Me*.

MOIRA BUFFINI
MATT CHARMAN
PENELOPE SKINNER
JACK THORNE

Greenland

faber and faber

First published in 2011
by Faber and Faber Ltd
74–77 Great Russell Street, London WC1B 3DA

Typeset by Country Setting, Kingsdown, Kent CT14 8ES
Printed in England by CPI Bookmarque, Croydon, Surrey

ISBN 978-0-571-27791-9

2 4 6 8 10 9 7 5 3 1

Greenland was first presented on the Lyttelton stage of the National Theatre, London, on 5 February 2011. The cast, in alphabetical order, included:

James Alper, Tobi Bakare, Natasha Broomfield, Elizabeth Chan, Michael Gould, Tamzin Griffin, Isabella Laughland, Amanda Lawrence, Tunji Lucas, Paul McCleary, Peter McDonald, Simon Manyonda, Lyndsey Marshal, Rhys Rusbatch and Sam Swann

Director Bijan Sheibani
Dramaturg Ben Power
Designer Bunny Christie
Lighting Designer Jon Clark
Video Designer Finn Ross
Music and Sound Dan Jones
Movement Director Aline David
Company Voice Work Jeannette Nelson, Kate Godfrey
Puppetry Mark Down

Characters

Adeel

Paula

Lisa

Shopper

Ray

Robert

Harold

Harry

Sarah

Freya

Al

Naval Cadet

Phoebe

Damien

Bernice

Natasha

Dav

Susie

Peta

Sam

Claude

Adam

Pam

Serena

Celia

Nigel

Alamir

Seydou

Depledge

Oppenheim

Jacobs

Waiter

Mac

GREENLAND

ONE

Darkness. Then, gradually, the company appear, with Adeel at the front of the stage.

Adeel They say your beliefs are determined by those around you. Did you know that? There's this thing actually. Proves it. Phenomenon. Shit, what's it called? Anyway I can't remember but it works like this. Say for example you're sitting in a room. And in the room are other people. I don't know how many. Doesn't have to be loads but enough. And the door to the room is closed. And at some point under the closed door comes smoke. Yeah? You can see smoke coming under the door. But instead of panic –
    instead of people getting up and jumping out the window or whatever –
    for some reason all the other people in the room say they can't see no smoke. Right? Well according to this phenomenon,
    in this situation you
    you yourself are highly likely
    even as the room is filling up with smoke you are highly likely to start believing the majority. By which I mean you don't just start saying you can't see the smoke because you want to agree with them. But if enough people say it
    you actually start to think they're right
    and you're wrong. Right? I'm not explaining it very well. It's like this: even if you can see and smell smoke
    if everyone else in the room denies it
    then you will most likely start to believe

3

that the smoke is not there. Thas just normal human behaviour. We all do it. But once you know –

this is the amazing thing. Once you know about the phenomenon? Part of the phenomenon is that once you know about it? *Then* you become less likely to

whatsit

succumb to it. Yeah? If you understand your own condition

then when you see the smoke

whatever the other people say

you keep thinking: I see smoke. And *then* you become more likely to call it out! And see

thas what my mum taught me. To have the courage of my own conviction. To speak out. Regardless to the majority or what they think. I'm never gonna sit in a room and not see that smoke, yeah? I'm calling it out. I'm just saying all this to let the banker know. Mr Banker? This is who you're up against, yeah? I'm a leader. I'm a thinker. I'm a gambler. And I may be a little guy

but I'm ready to take down Goliath. I'm ready to play. Let's go!

TWO

The company try and respond to a series of climate-based quiz questions. They don't know the answers. Music and a large amount of plastic falls from above. The company scatter it about the space. Lisa enters, sitting in a shopping trolley which floats over the heads of the company, who become supermarket shoppers. Paula enters.

Paula Lisa, what are you doing in here?

Lisa Nothing.

Paula You hate supermarkets.

4

Lisa I know.

Paula I've never seen you with a trolley in my life.

Lisa Mum –

Paula I wish I'd known you were coming, I'd have given you a list.

Lisa I want to leave my course.

Paula What?

Lisa My PGCE. I'm not going to finish it.

Paula Lisa – what's happened?
   Are you pregnant?

Lisa No.

   Lisa hands Paula a book.

Paula *Climate Wars* – 'The Fight for Survival as the World Overheats'.
   What's this?

Lisa I don't know what to do.

Paula Finish your course.

Lisa I can't.

Paula Why not?

Lisa Because . . .
   Ipswich might drown.

Paula Oh for heaven's sake. When?

Lisa It's like we're conducting this massive experiment, a big huge experiment and all we know is it will make our world go hotter. Mum, the ice is melting and I'm really, really scared.

Paula So
   Why are you in the supermarket?

Lisa This is a protest.

Paula Are you in here shoplifting?

Lisa No, look at the packaging.

Paula Don't leave your teaching course.

Lisa Everything we eat is wrapped in plastic.

Paula Yes but we recycle.

Lisa There's a plastic island in the Pacific.
And it's now the size of France.

Paula Lisa, plastic doesn't heat the planet.

Lisa takes a bunch of roses from a trolley.

Lisa Look at these roses, Mum.

Paula They're beautiful.

Lisa They fly them here from Kenya.
It's summer.
There are roses growing in the car park right outside.

Paula But they've got bugs in them.

Lisa *(from her own trolley)* These beans are from Peru.
Lamb from New Zealand.
Strawberries from Spain.
How many planes – just to bring us our shopping?
How much CO_2?
These roses are so perfect –

Lisa starts to tear the heads off them.

But this is what they're doing to the atmosphere.

Paula Is this your protest?

Lisa Yes.

Paula I don't think people understand.

Lisa I'm sorry, everyone, but I'm protesting.
  Cos the way we shop is mad.

Paula Sweetheart
  All this eco stuff is making you unhappy.

Lisa If we all did this –
  If we all filled trolleys full of over-packaged flown-in
goods –
  And left them as a protest once a week –
  Sixty million people saying no, we don't need this –
  The supermarkets would all stop
  And Ipswich wouldn't drown.

Shopper Ipswich isn't going to drown.

Lisa Not in your lifetime,
  But when that baby over there is old
  This supermarket might be sea.

Paula Lisa, if the supermarkets stopped, what would we
eat?

  Beat.

Come home.

Lisa Why aren't you afraid, Mum?

Paula I am, love.
  I am.

  *Lisa flies up and off as Dr Ray Boykin appears among
  the shoppers. He steps forward.*

Ray Thank you. For inviting me here. Before I begin my
lecture, I wanted to start with a couple of jokes about
climate change. Just to break the ice . . .

  No response. Someone coughs.

How about this one? 'Turns out the only high ground in
the Maldives is the moral high ground.' . . . You see, it's

only 1.5 metres above sea level, which is rising, of course. At 0.9 cm a year. So there is no high ground, you know . . . to speak of . . .

An excruciating silence. He stares out.

I'm gonna push through to the science I think. (*Clearing his throat.*) Figure one, please.

The 'hockeystick graph' appears behind him. As the temperature line rises dramatically, so does Lisa, who is now floating above the stage.

Most of you will no doubt recognise this. The diagrammatic you're looking at is known to the climate community as the hockeystick graph. It was constructed using temperature estimates from the past thousand years. Its emergence in 1998 as the first quantitative hemispheric-scale reconstruction shows a sharp rise in temperatures during the second half of the twentieth century. Relatively flat to 1900, the 'shaft' of the stick, followed by a sharp increase analogous to the 'blade'. This is what first made me want to study the climate, over a decade ago. I'd been a pure biologist until that point. This piece of evidence changed my life . . . convinced me of our effect on the planet, since the dawn of the Industrial Revolution.

Announcement It's been disputed, of course . . .

Ray I'm sorry?

Announcement It's been contested. The graph. The statistical methods used to build it. A Congressional Committee was set up in the US.

Ray A panel of scientists convened by the National Research Council, who agreed there were some statistical failings, but that it had little or no effect on the result. Over a dozen successive scientific papers, using a variety of statistical techniques, produced reconstructions virtually identical to the original hockeystick. This has been the warmest decade in a thousand years and it's our fault.

Announcement Tell us about climate modelling.

Ray (*beat*) Well . . . what do you want to know?

Announcement Do you have faith in the current climate models that exist?

Ray *Faith?* No. Three years ago my team and I began building a new kind of climate model. Except with ours – full dynamic process-based – I believe we'll most accurately be able to predict the future climate of the next hundred years. Figure 97 please.

The diagram behind Ray changes to show NASA satellite imagery of the Arctic ice.

Recently published data collected from NASA satellites supports the hypothesis that once an ice sheet starts to disintegrate, it can reach a tipping point beyond which break-up is explosively rapid. Figure 98 please. If this entire sheet was to melt it would contribute 4.8 metres to global sea level. The only question is when . . .

Climate science has been completely dominated for the past fifty years by physicists. That's why there's little or no biology in the models. That's what I'm trying to address. We are now engaged in a game of 'wait and see'. Our eyes trained on the ice like a slumbering giant, waiting for it to wake. Terrified what'll happen when it does.

Harry enters and slowly walks forward, looking through binoculars. He is dressed in modern Arctic gear. Ray exits as the lights change.

THREE

A Cambridge don's study emerges. Robert and Harold enter.

Robert Harold, right?

Harold Yes, sir.

Robert Sit where you choose.

Harold looks around. Robert smiles wryly.

There's no test in which chair you pick.

Harold thinks and then sits. Robert reads through the pages in front of him.

You're from Walthamstow?
I once went to the dog track in Walthamstow.

Robert reads more.

We don't have a huge amount of grammar-school boys here, so that might be intimidating . . . Do you think you'll be able to cope?

Harold I've never been good at fitting in. I'll not fit in here just fine.

Robert (*laughs*) Novel answer.

Beat. Robert looks inquisitively at Harold.

My big question is – always is – why, Harold? Why – Geography?

Harold Well. Um. The first person to use the word 'geography' was Eratosthenes. It literally translates from the Greek *geographia* as 'description of the earth's surface' –

Robert Harold, I don't mean to stop you mid-flow, but is your father one of those – encyclopedia salesmen? Because I assure you one thing I don't need is the *Britannica* definition of geography.

Harold My father's in post offices, sir. He runs a post office in Walthamstow.

Robert looks, turns and begins to exit.

Robert I'll make this easy. You applied for Geography because you thought you'd get in. You're a working-class boy on the make, part of me admires that. (*His voice tails off over the following text.*) Geography is a comparatively new subject for Cambridge – well, 1888, ergo a comparatively easy subject to crack . . .

Robert fades off as Harold stands and walks in a low arc behind and towards Harry. His chair disappears as he steps into the Arctic.

Harold Harry . . .

Harry doesn't answer.

What you looking for?

Harry doesn't hear.

Harry. What you looking for?

Harry doesn't hear.

Harry . . . Harry . . .

Harry Sorry?

Harry unwraps an ear.

Harold What you looking for?

Harry Bears.

Harold Bears?

Harry has more of a cockney accent than Harold – or he's making less of an effort to hide it. It's not heavy, but it's there.

Harry Some Inupiat Eskimos near Barrow had to kill a bear who wandered into the whaling camp . . .

Harold Polar bears come into the camps?

Harry is back looking through his binoculars.

Harry That's the negative way to look at that information.

Harold What's the positive?

Harry One less bear.

Harold digests this. Harry indicates something.

That's bear.

Harry returns to his tent and pulls out a canvas bag into the snow. He empties the bag. Inside are thirty three-foot high garden stakes. Harold stays looking at the ground where Harry pointed.

Harold What's bear?

Harry The seal vertebrae. That. You can see the chew marks. We'll be fine. Best we get the fence up, though. Before we get too tired. The guillies aren't arriving today. That's for sure.

Harold looks at the seal vertebrae.

Don't worry. We've got the mace and my *Screamer Banger*. We'll be fine.

Harold *Screamer Banger?*

Harry I was out here once and injured the tendon in my knee. Couldn't do anything but lie. Couldn't walk, couldn't stay warm. Kept thinking to myself – well, I'm prime meat now. But it didn't happen. Not once in – thirty-four – years has one so much as taken a nip.

Harold Good. That's good to know.

Harry They come through the wire, the wire triggers the mousetrap, the mousetrap triggers the car alarm. It's my own invention.

Harold And that'll scare them off?

Harry It definitely could. Though of course if they are hungry or a bit deranged, as they're all getting, and any and all meat will do, unlikely a car alarm will keep them out. Then it'll just be a way of letting us know we're about to be eaten.

Harold Couldn't – shouldn't – we build a bigger fence?

Harry There's not much you can do to keep Charles Manson out of the suburbs. Still, price you pay, for coming out here . . .

Harold Yeah.

Pause. Harry thinks. He flexes his arm as if getting the cold out of it.

Harry And, you know, life is about the things you're scared of.

Harold Yeah.

Harry I'm pleased you're here, kid.

Harold Yeah.

They look out at the ice. Freya appears. Looks at the ice. Harold and Harry exit.

FOUR

Sarah joins Freya and they talk to the audience.

Sarah The neighbour's dog. That's what started it. Well, no. Not exactly. It started when she went on her trip – (It started when you went on your trip / didn't it darling?)

Freya Yes.
   Yes.

Sarah That's when it started. But most recently the neighbour's dog has, well, exacerbated the situation.

Freya A dog. Does not need a light left on at night.

Sarah It's / a puppy.

Freya A dog. Is an animal.

Sarah A golden / retriever.

Freya A dog. Is not scared of the dark.

Sarah It's scared of the dark.

Freya It's a dog!

Sarah Don't shout!

Freya Sorry.

Sarah She stands at the bathroom window. For hours. Don't you?

Freya Counting.

Sarah Watching. Counting the hours till they turn it off.

Freya Eleven. Twelve.

Sarah Because it's not an environmentally friendly light bulb, see, and then they get up and the wife –
   What's her name?

14

Freya I can't / remember.

Sarah Well, anyway, the wife goes out to the garden with it and it does its toilet / and she –

Freya – and she picks it up / in a plastic bag!

Sarah – in a plastic bag.
  Yes.

Freya People in this country. The people of this country –

Sarah Darling.

Freya – don't give a flying shit.

Sarah I think that's a bit –

Freya What? The majority of the population of this country –
  Don't give a flying shit. Fact.

  Sarah and Freya dissolve away as Al and Paula enter.

FIVE

Lisa floats high above her parents.

Al If you want a cause, pick something proper.
  Pick poverty or AIDS or cruelty to dogs.

Lisa Not the destruction of our planet?

Al Are you really going to leave your course because these liars –
  Because these science fascists who are very well paid –
  And these bunny-hugging eco monsters
  Terrorists
  Are telling you the world is going to end?
  I can tell you categ-flipping-gorically it's not.

Lisa What's the point of being a teacher, Dad?

Paula You've always wanted to teach.

Lisa This is the biggest crisis we've ever faced.
And I'm standing there teaching PE?

Paula Don't waste your degree, Lisa.

Lisa I don't want to be a teacher any more.

Paula Well, what are you going to do?

Lisa I don't know.

Al Well, your life as an eco-warrior started really well.
Paula paying for a trolley full of torn-up goods.

Lisa You shouldn't have done that, Mum.

Paula They were calling the police.

Al It was bloody juvenile. How old are you?

Lisa About 1.9 million years.

Paula That's cheek, Lisa, and it won't help.

Al I mean, look at these books –
Storms of my Grandchildren.
Notes from a Catastrophe.
Climate Wars.
This is a campaign of fear.

Lisa It's science.

Al Global warming is a natural phenomenon. It's
happened again and again through geological time.

Lisa I know.

Al The planet has been far hotter than this.

Paula I'm sure there's been jungly type stuff right down
in the Antarctic, and wasn't there forest once all over
Greenland?

Al Change is what the climate has always been doing.

Lisa Not this fast.

Al It's like you've been brainwashed.

Lisa No, Dad, you have been brainwashed. /
The oil industry is paying huge amounts of money to
stop this urgent message getting through.

Al The world might be getting warmer but it isn't going
to / harm us.
Two degrees more would actually be good for us.

Lisa The people who insisted that the earth was flat
Because a globe shape threatened them –
Were they right? /
The earth is not flat.

Al Your information is incorrect.

Lisa Science was right then.
And it's right now.

Al The world is not about to end.

Lisa No, the world will go on.
It's us.
If we do nothing, we will end.

Paula Bringing you up has made us happy every day.
You've been a gift to us, you know that.

Lisa Mum, I wish I were still ignorant.
But I can see
From the bottom of the ocean to the stratosphere.

Al I would like to sue those sods for doing this to you
Those liars with their climate change –

Paula That's a hell of a burden, Lisa.

Al Those emails sent from Exeter –

Lisa East Anglia.

Al They proved it was all lies.

Lisa They didn't.

Al Yes, they did.
  They proved it was all
  They
  They proved –

Lisa I'm sorry.

*The stage is rocked by a huge explosion. Lisa flies off
as the whole company rush on to the stage.*

SIX

*The din from a whole armada now fills the air as a naval
battle explodes across the stage. A young Cadet takes
measurements in the midst of the chaos.*

Naval Cadet (*methodically as he writes*) HMS *Minotaur*.
Twenty-first day of October, eighteen hundred and five.
Captain, Charles John Moore Mansfield. Crew 74, three
killed, 22 injured. Position 36 degrees 17 35 North,
6 degrees 15 19 West. Cape Trafalgar, Spanish Coast.
(*He takes a breath and checks his instruments.*) At one
p.m. Wind East North East. Gale force 9 (*Looking up.*)
And cloudy. Temperature 14 degrees Celsius.

*He shuts the instrument box and waits, still clutching
the logbook. In a cessation of the cannon fire he
suddenly ups and runs over to where a man sleeps in
a blue sleeping bag. There is another sleeping bag, set
slightly back. The Cadet tucks the logbook under the
sleeping man's arm. Suddenly the strip lights blink on
and we're no longer on the deck of a ship but in a lab
in Exeter – work terminals and computers.*

Phoebe Dr Boykin?

Clutching the logbook, a disorientated Ray suddenly sits bolt upright. The Cadet is gone and now Phoebe Hammond stands watching him. She has keen eyes and a shoulder bag stuffed with documents. She holds out a steaming paper cup of coffee, watching him closely.

I stuck my head in a few minutes ago, but you were out cold. I did a lap of the building, bought you a coffee. Your PA said I should just wake you . . .

Silence. He stares, unsure whether he's still dreaming. She guesses he's forgotten.

We've been emailing.

Ray (*clearing his throat*) Flirty emails?

Phoebe You said you had something to show me. We arranged to meet. This morning. I got the first train down.

Ray (*remembers*) I'm really sorry. We pulled an all-nighter.

Phoebe We sleep over in the Commons sometimes. Jack Straw comes round and tucks us all in. Here . . .

Phoebe steps over to Ray and hands him the coffee. Only then does she spot the other sleeping bag. She looks surprised.

Ray Martin. My software engineer. Don't worry. He'll sleep through anything. Watch . . . (*Aiming this at his sleeping colleague.*) Martin? Martin? Martin. Martin. Martin – See.

She smiles and reaches out her hand awkwardly. He reaches out from his crumpled sleeping bag and shakes it.

Phoebe Phoebe Hammond. Department of Energy –

Ray – and Climate Change. You work for Ed Miliband. Ray Boykin.

Phoebe I know who you are.
   I came to your lecture on microbial communities – you cleared the room.

Ray OK. Well, that was a disaster. (*Beat.*) I got a bit flustered.

Phoebe I think you got a bit cocky.

Ray It happens when I get flustered.

Phoebe You made some pretty bold statements . . . Said you thought the current models that existed were incomplete. That you were working on something that could fill in the blanks.

Ray We are.

Phoebe A global model country by country up to 2100.

Ray I always do this. Email late night when I'm horny. Look, I just was just trying to impress you.

Phoebe Well, it worked. Here I am.

> *Ray wearily climbs out of his sleeping bag, wearing only a creased shirt and boxer shorts. Phoebe looks away demurely as he puts on his trousers.*

Look, there's a major briefing this afternoon. We're pulling together the final thoughts for Copenhagen . . . (*Her BlackBerry bleeps and she answers the email.*) It's been two years of work and suddenly people are panicking about whether it's gonna be a success out there. If an agreement is possible, you know, so we just might need new ammunition, new science to . . .

Distracted, she forgets what she's saying and looks at him. He's dressed now and sipping his coffee. He watches her and waits.

What was I . . . ?

Ray You were saying you need new science.

Phoebe (*worried*) I seem to be doing that more and more lately.

Ray Losing your train of thought?

Phoebe Yeah.

Ray Maybe your brain is starting to atrophy. Do you have problems remembering dates? Names?

Phoebe Sometimes.

Ray That can point to pretty rapid neuro-degeneration. How old are you, Phoebe?

Phoebe Thirty-two. (*Anxious.*) Are you serious?

Ray (*smiles*) I'm joking. You're just knackered, right? I know I am. I feel buried in here. Then when you do sleep you have the strangest dreams, all this shit floating round your head.

Phoebe I don't dream.

Ray You don't?

Phoebe I don't sleep. I was on the 5.30 from Paddington because you promised me science . . .

She looks at him hard. Ray gets the message, thinks and then hands her the logbook. She takes it carefully as he heads over to the computer.

HMS *Minotaur*?

Ray Fought in the Nile and then Trafalgar. Wrecked in 1810, but this showed up in a museum in Texel.

ul.

Boats, going right back into the
ry taking weather readings. Their ships
e world.

ng) 'Cape Trafalgar, Spanish Coast. At one
p.m.   ıst North East . . . Temperature 14 degrees
Celsius . . . (*Quietly.*) They were still recording the
weather in the middle of a battle?

Ray Down the corridor we've got 300 million separate
measurements that help build a picture of the last
hundred and fifty years of climate history. Early writings
on meteorology from the Royal Society, Robert Boyle's
diaries describing cloud cover. There's a guy counting
black guillemots in Alaska. Has been for thirty-five
years. Sent us records stretching back to the seventies.

Phoebe Why?

Ray Birds are the most studied thing on the planet and
most of the data comes from watchers. If we know what
used to be happening in the world then we can start to
piece together the effect we've had on the climate –

Phoebe And, what the future will look like.
So . . . show me the future.

*He gestures towards a nearby laptop, connected up to
a super-processor. Phoebe walks over to it and stares
at the screen. Her smile fades a little. She looks
confused.*

What is it?

Ray My model.

Phoebe The screen's blank.

Ray We're running a new variable. A new layer of data.
It takes the computer time to generate that.

Phoebe Right . . .

Ray That's why we slept the night. Each time you add a layer of data there are millions of possible combinations for it to churn through. Population growth, eight, nine or ten billion. GDP growth, phosphate shortages which are the basis of most of the planet's food production –

Phoebe How long?

Ray Two and half more minutes.

Phoebe And you haven't seen it yet?

He shakes his head.

What will it show? Can you summarise it for me?

Ray Summarise it?

Phoebe You've only added one variable, you must know roughly what it's going to show . . .

Ray This is three years of my life. You want a summary?

Phoebe You're trying to predict what the world is going to look like in the next hundred years, but those models already exist. I've seen them.

Ray You haven't seen my model.

He stares at Phoebe, who realises he hasn't said this for effect. He looks at his watch.

Phoebe So . . .? What's unique about it? What's it gonna show me I haven't already seen.

Ray I said in my lecture.

Phoebe Not really . . . (*Beat.*) Look, Professor –

Ray Doctor.

Phoebe Whatever. You invited me down here. That must have been for a reason.

Ray I think I'd rather not show you.

Phoebe What?!

Ray What are you gonna do with it? This information.

Phoebe Use it, if we can. If we need to.

Ray As leverage? In Copenhagen . . . Our work here is a scientific enquiry, it's not political.

Phoebe Everything's political. You work for us.

Ray I don't.

Phoebe You're state-funded.

Ray This information is not ready for the public domain.

Phoebe You invited me down here.

Ray It hasn't been peer-reviewed.

Phoebe That could take years.

Ray Yes, it does. Look, given time, science can do anything.

Phoebe Excuse me?

Ray And that's precisely because we're cautious, because we're careful.

Phoebe I'm standing here asking – no, fuck it, begging to see your model. To know if what you've got here is a game-changer, or just another model like all the rest. So which is it? Why won't you show me?

Ray Honestly? Because I'd rather not scare you.

She bursts out laughing but stays staring at him. After a moment her laughter subsides and she falls silent, pensive. We hear a ping. They look to the computer. Beat.

Phoebe I want to see it.

Ray doesn't budge. Phoebe is seething now.

Thank you. For wasting my fucking time.

Ray Stop talking about two degrees. The fight to limit global warming to easily tolerated levels is over. In Copenhagen you ought to be talking about 3.5 degrees by 2100. That's all I can tell you.

Phoebe looks at him for a moment and then leaves.

Martin!

Martin sits bolt upright as loud house music explodes across the lab. It transforms itself into . . .

SEVEN

An eco-festival. Night. It is raining. Lisa is among the protesters. A DJ and a singer. Dancing under the night sky. Lisa is on the phone to Al.

Al Lisa?

Lisa Hi Dad!

Al You don't have to worry.

Lisa I'm not worrying.

Al Nigel Lawson says it's absurd to think we can know what the world will look like in a hundred years, any more than the Edwardians could have predicted the internet. We can't know!

Lisa That's nice, Dad.
It must be comforting to think that.

Al Lisa.

Lisa I love you.

Al Where are you?

Lisa I'm here!!

She puts her phone down. She lets herself go. After a moment the music cuts out and we're in a tent at dawn. Lisa. Damien. Susie. Dav. Bernice. Peta.

Damien If we want change, we all have to be climate protesters.
This is the tent that could change your future,
The tent that could save ours.

Susie We believe that ordinary people can make change. And Damien – I know he won't sing his own praises, but – he's done *so much*.

Lisa Why are there only twelve people here?

Damien Twelve is a decent start.

Lisa I can't believe there's only twelve people. I mean, this festival's supposed to be full of people who care about the climate. It's why I came.

Damien Well, it's early yet.

Bernice Jonathan Cainer's on in the tent next door.

Natasha Who?

Bernice He does the horoscopes in the *Daily Mail*.

Peta And *Hello* magazine. So completely packed to the gills I couldn't even get in.

Susie Well, he might have the numbers but we have got the quality – that's how I see it.

Peta That's very empowering.

Damien We have got some very hands-on action planned
And we'd be thrilled if you took part.

Peta You know, this is actually so random because it's like probably destiny or something that I'm here. Like some kind of ironic confluence of planets that I couldn't get into Jonathan Cainer. Because this is the two things I care about most – me and the climate – sort of totally joined up.

Susie Some people want to talk about their horoscope and that's fine.
  But you want to change the climate.

Damien We're not lawbreakers, we're responsible citizens concerned about our future.

Susie We're on the brink of such exciting change. A global agreement on greenhouse gas emissions is within our grasp –

Damien The world's power is going to be converging on Copenhagen –

Dav Excuse me, look.
  I am actually an activist.
  Full-time.
  And whatever you say here
  It's very well meaning, but I hope you realise where the real fight is.

Lisa What do you mean?

Dav For the first time in history we're sharing,
  All of us, a global ideology.
  The system that thinks we can have infinite growth on a finite planet
  And until we find another paradigm –

Susie Sorry, but are you an anarchist?

Dav No, I'm just saying –

Susie Because they're on at two.

We're going to take our protest right to the heart of government.

Dav The struggle is now with corporations and not government; multinationals and oil. They're bigger than a lot of countries now. There's no transparency; they've no responsibility to anyone except their shareholders and they are all carbon-polluters. We've got less than ten years until we reach a tipping point.

Bernice Nothing will change unless there's a binding global treaty.
    That's where the struggle is, OK?

Damien Tell them what we got planned, Suze.

Susie OK. Out there in front of the Copenhagen conference,
    In the freezing Danish winter –
    While the cameras of the world are on us –
    We're going to show them what it means to be a human.

Damien No matter how cold it gets
    We're going to show the vulnerability of the naked human.
    A bare, forked animal in a harsh environment.

Lisa Naked?

Susie We are going to be out there
    In the cold
    To stop the heat.

Damien In the Cold to Stop the Heat!

Everyone In the Cold to Stop The Heat!

    They follow Damien and Susie out, except for Dav and Lisa.

Lisa So you're an activist.
What do you do?

Dav At the moment?
Food.
Are you coming?

She follows him off as the lights change.

EIGHT

Voice (*recorded*) 'You have reached the O2 voicemail messaging service. Please leave your message after the tone.'

A loud tone. Ray steps forward and leaves Phoebe a message.

Ray OK . . . So maybe you don't need protecting, but you do need softening up.
Before I tell you.
That is if you still want to know what the model shows and I didn't piss you off beyond all reason before . . .
We play this game in the lab sometimes, it's called Worst Case Scenario. We come up with extreme things, unlikely things. Kind of unthinkable, but it helps to consider them. It helps me, anyway. You ready? I'll start . . . (*He thinks.*) So American and Russian nuclear submarines, on routine patrol in the North Sea, collide, causing the world's largest ever nuclear blast and a tidal wave that lays waste to Holland and the Low Countries completely. It helps to imagine these things. Believe me. Try it.

A loud voicemail tone and Phoebe steps forward, leaving a message. She hesitates.

Phoebe I got your message . . . and after careful consideration I've decided to play your warped little game. (*Beat.*) The Queen is killed by a suicide bomber in a rogue faction of Fathers for Justice called the Real Fathers for Justice. No one can believe it . . . How's that? Unimaginable enough for you? Look, whether you like it or not, Dr Boykin, we're on the same side. So, if you want to be part of the solution, tell me what the fucking model shows you.

Voicemail tone.

Ray Dear Potty-mouth, nice try, but you're gonna have to do better than that. Kim Jong-Il challenges Barack Obama to a fist fight. He accepts. If Obama wins, North Korea will surrender its nuclear weapons and instal democracy. If Jong-Il wins, America must pay a trillion dollars. The fight is televised.

Music and the lights change and we're back . . .

NINE

Night at the eco-festival. Lisa and Dav alone.

Dav There's tons of shit that can be done.

Lisa What like?
Because I've felt powerless about all this, really paralysed.
It fucked me up.

Dav This problem will be solved by us, by people,
I genuinely think that.

Lisa We haven't got any power.

Dav Look at the third runway –
The people living round Heathrow stopped it.
We've got loads of power,
Especially in this country,

If we think something's wrong
We can say so without getting tortured or being killed.

Lisa So how do I get to be an activist?

Dav You act.

Lisa Those people, Damien and Susie and the rest –
they're protesters. I mean they've got jobs or kids and
then on a Saturday they protest. Which is fine, but I
want to do more than that. You do it as a job, don't
you?

Dav I wouldn't recommend it as a career – not if you
want stuff. Everything I own fits in a bag.

Lisa So who do you work for?

Dav I'm between organisations at the moment.
    But the small ones are the best.

Lisa That's not what I've heard. I'm Lisa. Have you got
a name?

Dav Dav.

Lisa Short for Dave?

Dav Short for Dafydd.

Lisa So what do we do, Dav?

Dav We?

Lisa To act.
    To make them stop destroying the air we breathe.

Dav You're, um –
    Forgive me but you're –
    You seem really nice and –

Lisa Fuck off.
    I'm serious.

Dav What if you get arrested?

Lisa What if we've only got ten years, like you said?

Dav Look, we might have twenty, maybe thirty if we're lucky. No one, not even those technocrat science wankers can see the future.

Lisa But Jonathan Cainer can, and he says –

Dav What does he say?

Lisa He says make hay
    While the sun fries.

Dav Does he?

    Lisa nods.

You know what no one tells you about being an activist?

Lisa What?

Dav It's massive fun.

    They are kissing. They dance off.

TEN

Adeel appears at the front of the stage. He holds a red 'Deal or No Deal' box. Behind him, a line of other players.

Adeel My mum
    She's kind of the reason I came on the show. You know? Cos it's like I put in my application yeah, I had bit of a rough start in life. Not saying thas unusual cos it ain't but my dad –
    I mean my mum brought me up on her own cos he was like –
    Can I say this? He was into drugs and all that? So we haven't really –

We'd like to get out from where we're from. See the world a bit. Go places. Do things. Maybe live somewhere you know where you don't have to look over your shoulder the whole time? Somewhere a bit more safe. She said,

Mum said: whatever you do, don't end up with a one-box game, Adeel. It's too big a risk. You can't stake your whole future on just one solution, know what I mean? But at the end of the day –

this is the thing about me, yeah? And I think it's because of my dad,

Cos of what he was like. I'm a risk-seeking individual. I'm always gonna gamble. Thas my nature. I'm like genetically incapable of being . . .

what's the word?

Frugal. For example. See, when there's a whole toilet roll? I use loads.

But then, when there's hardly any toilet roll left? I use one sheet at a time. Less. If I need to. And when it's all run out and I'm sat there thinking shit, what the fuck am I gonna do now? I remember all that toilet roll I used before. Just

rolling it off the thing like I'm an Andrex puppy, yeah? And I say to myself,

Remember this, Adeel. Next time use less. Last longer. But then when Mum's been to the shop and there's a whole roll again? I use loads. I don't even remember until next time it's all gone. And I don't know why? But I think it's because at the end of the day it's hard to think about the future, you know? Because

what if just after you buy a new roll

the world ends? You know? I coulda spent my last days using as much as I like. Why get shit on your hand if you don't need to? You know? Why am I talking about toilet rolls? Oh yeah. What I'm saying is this: there's no guarantees in this life. You can't live for tomorrow. I'm asking you:

What's the point of even thinking about probability
When you only get one chance to play the game?
Know what I mean?
You got to live
Right here, right now. Or at least. Thas my attitude.
So . . .
Yeah. I'm ready for the question.
Eleven thousand pounds . . .
(Oh shit,)
No deal.

The players cheer and race off. Sarah and Freya are left.

Sarah She says she finds it hard because other people haven't seen what she saw. Other people think –
   and I've said it myself so I don't mean in a bad way – but other people say:

Freya 'It's just ice.'

Sarah We were arguing. I wanted to flush the toilet and Freya said –

Freya If it's yellow / let it mellow.

Sarah I wasn't going to.

Freya If it's brown –

Sarah Freya! I don't think Helen wants to hear the rhyme.

Freya She might find it useful. Why don't we ask her?

Sarah No! / This isn't –

Freya Why not?

Sarah Because what did we agree? We're talking about our relationship. This is our time. Our space. To talk about us. Not the fucking climate. For once. OK?

34

Beat.

Freya Sorry.

Sarah She says it's difficult because other people haven't seen the ice. And she has. And I say it's difficult because I haven't seen the ice and sometimes I find it hard to make the connection between the ice –
  Which I do believe in –
  And the world.

Freya She / always says this.

Sarah Which is sort of –
  What?

Freya 'I do believe in.'

Sarah What do you mean?

Freya Like it's fairies.

Sarah No.

Freya Like we might wake up tomorrow and it's all been a dream.

Sarah See, this is what happens: I try and talk about my feelings / and she jumps –

Freya How is that / your feelings?

Sarah – into one about my terminology.

Freya How is that your feelings?

Sarah I feel guilty.

Freya Here we go.

Sarah I work in a school. OK? In Peckham. It's hard work. I do my best. When Freya told me about the meat I was a vegan for three months.

Freya She still ate cheese.

Sarah One time! Anyway, shut up. I'm telling Helen about my feelings. And on my way to the tube I pass a Starbucks. I don't –

I mean

I know Starbucks is bad. No one doesn't know Starbucks is bad. But they do really good coffee. And in the winter –

Before I met Freya –

I used to walk past that Starbucks and on a Friday morning

I'd go in. To say well done to myself for getting through the week. Warm me up. Make me feel –

Freya Friday morning?

Sarah It was my weekly treat.

Freya She went in every day.

Sarah No.

Freya Yes you did.

Sarah Freya!

Freya She does something once

And she tells herself as she does it 'just this once' and it's like

Because she says that every time somehow her brain manages to convince her that it's true.

Sarah Helen has no idea what you're talking about.

Freya This is a woman who smoked twenty a day

For ten years

And when I suggested to her she might like to give up? What did you say?

Sarah I gave up last year.

Freya 'I'm not a smoker.'

Sarah I'm not.

36

Freya Because every time she had a fag it was 'just this once'.

They disappear. As wind blows and a campfire sparks into life.

ELEVEN

Harry and Harold sit round the fire. The sky is dark, but not black. The fire burns high. The sparks fly loud and proud. They have taken off goggles and hats. They look warmer. Harold looks up at the sky. Harry is on a radio.

Harry Mac . . . Mac . . . Mac . . .
Mac. Come in, Mac. I need a food drop and a – I need to arrange pick-up.

No reply. He puts the radio down. Harry stares into the flames. Then he looks up at the sky. Then he stares into the flames.

Harold Will the guillemots come tonight?

Harry They may do. They'll come . . . then they'll go . . . and then they'll come again.

Harold They'll fly by?

Harry smiles. He looks up at the sky. And then down at the ground.

Harry They'll fly by and gauge the degree of snow melt from the air – they're good at that. Snow melt right, they'll come, snow melt wrong, they won't. They come down too soon, they can't get in their nest cavities, well then, they'll be out against the snow. And you don't want to be a black thing against a white backdrop, that's just asking for trouble . . . I've seen the snowy owl take a few – not a pleasant sight.

Harold No.

Harry Then again – time it wrong – arrive too late – you risk losing your long-time mate. Imagine you have a girlfriend.

Harold looks at Harry uncertainly.

Harold Not so hard.

Harry Imagine knowing that you just have to hit the right time to keep her. But Valentine's Day – well, it shifts every year. You get the right time – marriage, house, kids, You get the wrong time – death or romantic oblivion. Time it too *late*, your girlfriend –

Harold Harry . . .

Harry – moved on to another man. David. Doing A-level Latin. Devilish smile. Just like that.

Harold Yes. Well. I don't –

Harry Or George. School football captain. Wonderful biceps.

Harold OK. You're just going to keep on with this so . . .

Harry Time it too *early* and you have your neck ripped out by a snowy owl.

Harold Good.

Pause. Harold looks back into the flames. He nervously asks his next question.

Are you . . . seeing anyone . . . at the moment . . . ?

Harry Sitting unpaid and alone on an island on the north-west tip of Alaska for three months in a year doesn't do wonders for your romantic life. A few have flown in and flown out again. No nesters.

*Harry thinks and then looks at Harold and smiles.
Harold doesn't smile.*

Harold OK. I know. You just love your birds.

Harry raises an eyebrow at him.

Harry Oh no. No no. That's a dangerous . . . uh . . .
I don't love birds. And if I did they'd be prettier than a
guillie. Uglier than a pigeon, I'd say. No, no, I don't love
the birds. I . . .

Harry hears something. He stands.

Harold What?

Harry Nothing.

*Harry is still looking. He sits. He warms his hands.
He hears something again. He stands again.*

Harold Have we any beer?

Harry We have vodka. Vodka doesn't freeze. Well,
vodka does freeze but only at 114 below . . . Ha!

Harold What?

*Harold stands and looks in the same direction Harry
is looking.*

Harry Ha.

Harold What? Stop saying 'ha'.

Harry Speak of the devils . . .

Harold I can't . . . see . . .

Harry You'll see.

Harold Oh.

*Eight birds fly overhead. Harry raises his hands to
them.*

Harry One, three – eight.

Harold That wasn't . . .

Harry Eight.

Harold They looked –

Harry They're having a nervous look.

Harold Are they . . . coming back . . .?

Harry Of course they're coming back!

Harold Right. Do I . . . Am I standing – looking – in the right direction . . .

Harry smiles at Harold. And then looks back at the sky.

Harry Here she blows!

Harold OK.

Harry He's having a dive . . .

A bird dives towards the ground.

He's having a think . . .

The bird pulls out of the dive. Harry laughs.

He's rethought.

They watch. Harry laughs.

He's rethought!

Harold There's more. Coming.

Harry Of course there's more! This is a party!

Harold A second flock.

Harry Twenty –

Harold The circles they're making –

Harry Twenty – maybe thirty –

Harold Rising. Dipping. Around and around. Fifty feet above the ground.

> *More birds fly overhead. And they're astonishing. It's an astonishing noise.*
>   *More birds dive-bomb. Harold is having the time of his life. Giggling. Jiggling. Having the time of his life. Harry watches him.*

Harold Harry. You want to know what you should love? This. This. A show. Just for us. I feel like I'm conducting the world.

Harry There's another flock. There's more.

> *Harold begins to dance. Harry laughs with delight. He's starting to get into it seriously.*

Harold Fifty. Eighty. Amazing. The greatest show on earth and we're the only ones who get to see it.

Harry I do love the way they keel –

Harold Yes.

Harry From black wing to white underwing.

Harold You are beautiful. Look. Look. Like a swirlpool.

Harry It is something.

Harold I'm conducting the world. Wooooo-hoooooo.

Harry They are something –

Harold Woooo-hooooo.

> *Harry looks at Harold with affection.*

Harry Wooo-hoooo.

Harold Will any land?

Harry Woo-hooo.

Harold Will any land?

Harry I'm sorry I called you pigeons. I'M SORRY I CALLED YOU PIGEONS. WOO-HOOOO.

Harold Harry, you're crying.

He is.

Harry I'm fine. Just happy to be – with you – tonight.

Harold Will any land?

Harry No. Not tonight. Tonight they're just here to dance.

And we watch as they watch, two people, a fire and eighty birds. It's magnificent.

TWELVE

Lisa is on the phone to Paula.

Lisa Mum, guess what?

Paula You're coming home.

Lisa I've met someone.

Paula That's nice.

Lisa He's amazing.
He like knows so much.
He's got a world view, Mum.

Paula Oh . . .

Lisa I'm working with him.

Paula What as?

Lisa I'm phoning up to say that if I get arrested –
Just don't worry.

Paula Lisa –

Lisa It'll be a really minor charge.

Lights snap up as Lisa and Dav enter an office. Lisa holds a video camera. They have hung a banner outside which reads: DANGER, TOXIC GREENWASH. *Claude, Sam, Adam (the boss), Pam, Serena and Celia.*

Lisa OK, ladies and gentlemen, we're sorry to interrupt your morning and intrude upon your workplace –

Claude What the heck –

Pam Who are you?

Dav We wouldn't do it unless it was a matter of life and death.

Sam What are you talking about?

Lisa We are non-violent –

Pam Where's security?

Dav We don't wish to cause harm to any person or any property –

Pam That's my desk – Hey – watch my stuff.

Lisa We don't wish to compromise your safety or security.

Dav *and* **Lisa** But we will be chaining ourselves to your desks until further notice.

Sam *(into phone)* Can you get up here?

Lisa We'd like to remind you of our right, under international law, to peaceful protest.

Dav We are here to highlight the devastating effect your work is having on the environment.

Claude What?

Adam How dare you?

Sam We've got climate wankers.

Lisa Please take a leaflet.
Don't be scared, we're non-aggressive.

Pam takes a leaflet.

Adam You're in the wrong place. We're environmental planners.

Dav Yes, we know.

Serena We are here making sure that oil companies do what they're supposed to do.

Dav Oil companies get oil and burn it – that's what they're supposed to do.

Lisa The oil companies are going further and deeper than they ever have before and I'm afraid your company is providing the greenwash.

Pam What do you mean, 'greenwash'?

Dav Spreading misleading information to conceal abuse of the environment.

Celia This is so depressing.

Lisa There's an oil and gas rush in the Arctic that will prove disastrous for our planet.

Dav You're doing studies on the environmental impacts of new deepwater drilling off the coast of Greenland –

Claude Look – the world needs energy, OK?

Pam And deepwater drilling has a very low impact on surrounding sealife.

Dav You're facilitating climate change.

Sam Oh, fuck off.

Claude We make it less bad.
  We make the whole thing less bad.

Dav What, killing pristine ecosystems in a less bad way?

Sam Security's going to be up here any minute.

Adam Let's take a break, people. Extremists never listen to reason and I don't see why we should listen to them.

Pam You're just going to leave them on their own in here?

Adam They've chained themselves to the desks. What can they possibly do?

Pam If you want something really environmentally devastating, one of our competitors is doing a study on the Canadian tar sands –

Sam Shut up, Pam.

  The others leave.

Lisa (*to Dav*) Did that go well? Because that was amazing – that was awesome.

Celia Tell her to turn the camera off.

Dav OK.

Celia I am not a villain.
  I resent the whole damn thing.
  I want to love my job.
  I've always wanted to believe we're doing good.

Dav I'm sorry if we're interfering with all that.

Celia I'm going to swear –

Dav Go right ahead.

Celia Fuck it.

OK really fuck and fucking fuck.
There's this project that you really ought to know about –
A gas pipeline in Papua New Guinea.

Dav OK.

Celia There are so many reasons why this thing could be calamitous. Our Environmental Impact Study is woefully, woefully inadequate.
These companies will suck oil and gas from every crevice in the earth.
I keep seeing burning animals
And archipelagos of infinitely colourful dead fish.
I'm not convinced it's safe.

Dav What's your name?

Celia Celia. You'll never stop them building it.

Dav But we can make it twice as hard.
Come on now, Celia, there's shitloads we can do.

Celia What about her? – She looks like a baby.

Lisa I've got a degree in Sports Science.

Dav She's fine.

Celia I'm going out there. I can give you the report and other documents –

Dav Amazing.

Celia If I set off along this path
You promise me one thing.

Dav Of course.

Celia Don't waste my fucking time.

They race off. Music and the office become an airport.

THIRTEEN

Phoebe, with a suitcase. She checks her voicemail.

Ray Facebook's 500 million users club together and pay off all of Africa's debt. America tries to re-impose the debt and shuts down Facebook.

Nigel enters behind Phoebe.

Nigel Not interrupting, I hope . . .

Phoebe turns, surprised. Nigel, a journalist, is staring at her.

Phoebe Nigel.

He has a flight bag over his shoulder. She hangs up the phone and automatically hands him a press release from a clear plastic folder. Nigel looks at it and then at her. A sense of occasion.

Nigel This is it then . . . Wanna sit together?

Phoebe We're on different flights.

Nigel How do you know?

Phoebe I made sure.

He smiles. He looks down at the press release. He reads it.

Nigel 'The European Union will be working to achieve maximum progress towards finalisation of an ambitious and legally binding global climate treaty to succeed the Kyoto Protocol in 2013 . . .' Tell me you didn't write this press release.

Phoebe What's wrong with it?

Nigel It doesn't crackle.

Phoebe Crackle?

Nigel For my readers.

Phoebe It's not fucking breakfast cereal, Nigel. A hundred and ninety-one world leaders are about to make history.

Nigel Whoa there!

Phoebe I mean it.

Nigel I'm sure you do but . . . you might just want to manage expectations a little. Unless you know something I don't. Am I about to report that we've saved the world . . .?

Phoebe's phone rings. She recognises the number: Ray. She smiles involuntarily and then remembers Nigel.

Distracted?

She switches the phone off.

Phoebe No.

Nigel What about a drink? Help you sleep on the plane.

Phoebe It's a fifty-minute flight.

Nigel Might be the last bit of rest you get for a fortnight. Don't worry, you're buying. Whack it on Ed's expenses . . .

And they walk through check-in and off. Alamir enters and introduces himself. He is in national dress. Seydou follows. He has opted for a western suit.

Alamir My name is Alamir Konate. This is my colleague, Seydou Diakite.

Seydou Hi.

Alamir We are engineers. We work for the Ministry of the Environment in Mali.

Seydou Tell them where that is.

Alamir Don't patronise them.

Seydou Mali is here.

A map appears.

Alamir We are on our way to a cold European capital.

Seydou Copenhagen.

Alamir I'm sure you know my country's position on climate change?

Seydou No, they won't. They won't know anything about us.

Alamir Of course they will. They are educated middle class.

Seydou What's our capital city?
  You see – no one knows.

Or:

Alamir No, that lady almost had her hand up.

Or:

Alamir That's right.
  Bamako, beautiful town on the banks of the Niger.
  And of course you've heard of Timbuktu.

Seydou They want to know how poor we are and what's going on with our climate.
  We're third poorest.
  Third poorest in the world.

Alamir On whose list?

Seydou On this list.
  Oxford University Multidimensional Poverty Index.

Alamir These lists don't tell you anything about us.

Seydou We are multidimensionally poor.

Alamir Our desert's growing by half a kilometre a year.

Seydou Rainfall is down by twenty per cent. Livestock is dying. People are starving. The Sahara is descending on our farmland.

Alamir I don't wish to depress them.
    People turn away when they're depressed.
    Please handle it more carefully, Seydou.

Seydou We don't have time.

Alamir We have a desert wind, the Harmattan, that blows down sand from the north. The Harmattan is coming every year for longer now and when it blows there's nothing you can do. Your skin dries, your lips bleed, the dust gets in your eyes and makes them red.

Seydou By 2025 two-thirds of all our farmland could be gone.

Alamir A rise of two degrees in global temperature –
    Just two degrees –
    Will bring – I'm sorry to upset you with this word –
    Will bring disaster to our people.

Seydou We have been preparing for this conference for two years.

Alamir Our democratic government has found the means to train and send a most impressive delegation.

Seydou Fifty of us.

Alamir More than Belgium.

Seydou Are you going dressed like that?

Alamir Of course.

Seydou To Copenhagen?

Alamir I'm proud to wear our national dress.

Seydou You'll freeze.

Alamir My friend, to freeze will be an interesting sensation.

They leave as Phoebe re-enters, ready to board her flight. A voicemail tone. Phoebe listens to the message.

Ray OK. You win. I expect . . . (*Thinking long and hard.*) the sixth mass extinction of life on the planet. The first in 65 million years. Half the species gone by the end of the century – a thousand times faster than you would expect from evolution. A global rise in temperature so acute the heatwaves buckle the ancient infrastructure of every city in Western Europe. I expect when your daughter's about thirty-five for the tarmac on her street to melt twice a year. I expect she'll need to teach her children how to use a gun. Do you want kids, by the way? (*Beat.*) I expect mainland Spain to be largely uninhabitable by the end of the century. And Suffolk to be fucked. But if you're buying a house, might I recommend the seaside, Somerset. As close to Hinkley Point nuclear power station as you can bear. If there's one coast they'll protect with their last breath it's going to be the area around a nuclear power station. If the sea defences get knocked down they'll be replaced the next day, even if other places are left to flood.

Phoebe, if we removed twenty of the micro-organisms in a healthy human body it would die. Yet we are removing twenty from the earth's ecosystem and expecting a different result. So personally, I expect to feel . . . endangered. (*Beat.*) Bear in mind it's a prototype. But after playing 'Worst Case Scenario', it doesn't feel quite so bad, right? To think about the unimaginable. I want a future. A family one day, so I have to do that . . . Safe journey.

Beat. Phoebe presses buttons on her phone. Voicemail tone and she leaves a message.

Phoebe Come to Copenhagen. Bring the model. You worked so hard on it, let it do some good now. There are tall buildings full of clever people that will think of ways to fix things if you ask them. Come out, Ray. We need you. You're my secret weapon. Besides, I've bragged to people about you. Bored Ed Miliband about what a find you are . . . I mean scientifically, you know. (*Beat. An announcement.*) Look it's final boarding. I've got to go. Think about it. But bring a jumper, they say it's fucking freezing.

FOURTEEN

A plane flies overhead, and we're at the end of a runway in Copenhagen.

Phoebe and the Copenhagen delegates dance. The music ends and Depledge steps forward.

Depledge My name is Joanna Depledge and I have worked for the UN secretariat for over fifteen years. We're the civil service of the regime, about three hundred, four hundred people strong, responsible for organising all the climate change negotiations. I suppose I do it because I like it. I met my husband whilst negotiating the Kyoto Protocol.

OK, so delegate arrives and the delegate has . . . quite a big delegation, probably about twenty-five or thirty people on her delegation, she needs to make sure that all those delegates – her delegation – are kept happy.

Alamir and Seydou emerge from the delegate group.

Alamir So here we are in our freezing European capital.

Seydou I know you are regretting national dress.

Alamir Not for a moment.
But I am regretting all the Danish fish in vinegar.

Seydou In Denmark there should be a dictionary full of words for cold.

The delegates queue for their badges and entry to the conference centre.

Depledge A very important thing they'll have to do is actually get their delegate badge. So you have to queue up in front of secretariat staff and show your credentials. Before that you can't enter into the building.

Seydou I'm going to get a chest infection here.

Seydou receives his badge and heads through security.

Alamir As delegates our passes will be pink.
Pink is the best.
The NGOs and journalists have colours of their own
And there are areas they cannot go.
The centre can hold fifteen thousand people,
There are forty thousand here I think.
After queuing for two long hours
At last we are inside.
We have been taught about the plenaries.

Seydou Big meetings – everybody there. Important stuff. There are all these different groups. G8, EU, G77, the LDCs –

Alamir That's us – the least developed countries.

Seydou There's AOSIS.

Alamir That's small island states –

Seydou The umbrella group, the OPEC countries, the rainforest states –

Depledge At the start of the negotiations everyone will have usually a big negotiating text, produced after the last negotiating session, based on the last session's work, and it will usually be a great big thing.

There are six UN languages – English, Chinese, French, Arabic, Spanish, Russian. Six languages.

The delegates become interpreters.

And everything is translated into English first. So if you speak French, that will be interpreted into English first and then, say, into Arabic.

The delegates form smaller groups.

The contact groups are smaller and discuss individual issues. They take place in the smaller meeting rooms.

Alamir I'm very glad we had our training. Because it is a –

Seydou Yes, it's like a –

Alamir Red-tape carnival.

Seydou Exactly.

Alamir All these different affiliations and these little deals and discussions going on in meetings and in groups and non-groups.

Seydou And in non-non-groups.

Alamir And the paper – talk about deforestation.
   There are papers and non-papers.

Seydou There are non-non-papers.

Depledge The contact group has its own particular chapter of this document that corresponds to its particular issue. Brackets are points of contention – anything we can't get agreement on, we put brackets round it. So you get a lot of different options represented in the document.

We see text, and Joanna and the company adding the brackets.

Depledge Problems with documents are an enduring feature in life generally. There have been a number of moments where the person who has written the text the night before gets to the documents counter, sees all the copies and thinks, 'Oh shit. There's a mistake.'

Alamir In the first week we've been told we just might get some sleep. It's harder for the LDCs because our hotels are not near the centre. The Americans can go upstairs and catch their power-naps.

Seydou Four hours in the first week and very little in the second.

Alamir Negotiation by exhaustion. This is real.

Seydou We are busy, busy, busy, morning, noon and night.

Alamir But we have hopes of respite pinned on Saturday – the delegations' football match, and then the NGO party.

Seydou We're hoping for some very decadent behaviour.

They slide back and the conference becomes a disco. Phoebe and the others dance awkwardly. Ray enters. He looks around, lost. Phoebe steps over and taps him lightly on the shoulder. Ray turns and looks at her. He smiles, she smiles back wider, a little tipsy. He opens a bag and pulls out a thick woollen jumper with the sales tag still attached. They shout to be heard.

Ray TOOK YOUR ADVICE. BOUGHT IT AT THE AIRPORT.

Phoebe VERY DASHING.

Ray I'VE BEEN LOOKING FOR YOU FOR HOURS. WHERE HAVE YOU BEEN?

Suddenly the music ends and people applaud. A ballad starts, quieter. People slow-dance. Ray and Phoebe seem shy now they don't have to shout.

Ray What is this place?

Phoebe Welcome to Middle Saturday. There's always an NGO party. Tomorrow's a day off. The last chance for people to sleep together.

Ray Right.

Phoebe A little sexual tension does wonders for climate negotiations come Monday morning.

Ray What happens Monday morning?

Phoebe's BlackBerry trills and she quickly fires back a message.

Phoebe (*distracted*) The high-level segment starts. Ministers arrive, leaders this time too: Gordon, Obama, Sarkozy.

Ray Have you met him? Obama . . .

Phoebe We've got a brush-by planned.

Ray A brush-by?

Her BlackBerry trills again. She passes him her glass so she can type two-thumbed.

Phoebe It's not really a meeting. He's only supposed to meet with Gordon, you know, officially, but Ed wanted a brush-by. A two-minute chat, if you're lucky, but they said yes, so . . . (*Getting her head straight.*) So I have to make sure Ed is ready to be brushed by at a moment's notice.

Ray OK.

Ray looks around and feels increasingly out of place. She looks up at him.

56

Phoebe Are you all right? Shall I get you a drink?

Ray (*hands the glass back to her*) I'm fine. I'm just suddenly feeling . . .

Phoebe What?

Ray Like I shouldn't have come. You've got enough going on.

Phoebe God no . . . Honestly, Ray, it's still up for grabs.

Ray You think?

Phoebe A deal is still possible. You brought it with you?

Still reluctant, Ray holds up his laptop bag.

Ray I've been watching people all afternoon. All these huddles, all these different groups. Different passes, different doors. I don't really get it, to be honest . . . All this. Paper and people.

Phoebe You should understand this better than anyone. Bunch of NGOs, journalists and politicians feeding on each other. It's a system, right? A microbial community.

Ray Is that what I'm looking at?

Her BlackBerry beeps. She looks at it and then looks up, glancing around.

Phoebe Fuck!

Ray What is it?

Phoebe We have to go. I've been spotted.

Ray By who?

Nigel (*off*) Sweetheart!

Phoebe Too late. Nigel!

Nigel saunters over.

Nigel Quick word? Very quick, I promise. May I?

Phoebe Shoot.

Nigel On the record.

Phoebe Always.

Nigel It's all going to shit, isn't it? The Chinese, Sudan, Brazil – they're pretty pissed off with L9.

Phoebe I don't know what you're talking about.

Nigel Really? The UK government didn't co-operate with twenty other governments to cook up an agreement in an attempt to supersede the 200-page version.

Phoebe 'The time to start planning is today, now, at Copenhagen. Before the crisis. Before the collapse. Before a catastrophe marks the point of no return. Before the options run out.'

Nigel Good. Punchy. I can use that.

Phoebe I'm quoting the *Wall Street Journal*.

Nigel Bitch. Dance with me.

Phoebe shakes her head. Nigel glances over at Ray.

Who's this . . .?

Phoebe He's not a child, why don't you ask him.

Ray Dr Ray Boykin.

Nigel Right. (*Looking at them.*) Is there something going on here? A sordid conference romance?

Phoebe Fuck off, Nigel.

Nigel You're still on the record. (*Beat.*) So . . . Dr Ray, let me guess . . . Geo-engineer? Nuclear scientist?

Phoebe Climate-modeller.

Nigel I see. And what does the world look like in fifty years?

Phoebe Apparently you're still a cock.

Nigel All right, all right! I get the message. I'll leave you to it.

Phoebe No! Actually stay. (*Remembering her BlackBerry.*) I've got to call the office. (*To Ray.*) Get a drink. (*To Nigel.*) Be nice.

She passes Ray her drink and kisses him on the cheek, leaving them. Surprised, Ray watches her go. He smiles, embarrassed. Nigel watches this jealously. Beat, and then Nigel offers Ray a cigarette. He declines, still clutching Phoebe's glass. Nigel smiles and smokes.

Nigel She's got a five-year career plan, you know. Great girl, very ambitious. So what do you think?

Ray Of Phoebe?

Nigel Of Copenhagen. A scientist's point of view . . .

Ray I couldn't comment. Honestly, I don't know what's going on here. I have no clue. I'm used to a lab. Order, process. This has neither of those things.

Nigel But now you're here to get your hands dirty? (*Beat.*) So who's seen your laptop?

Ray No one yet.

Nigel Wanna show me?

Ray I don't think I should.

Nigel You know – and take this in the spirit it's intended – but you scientists, you really ought to grow a bit of a backbone.

Ray A *bit* of a backbone? Which *bit* do you suggest?

Nigel Very witty. Very clever. I'm clever too and I would listen to you lot, but I think you're too scared to come out and tell us what you really think is happening. Why is that? Worried about losing your funding?

Ray It's because we don't know what's happening.

Nigel You know there's a problem.

Ray We don't know the scale of it.

Nigel But you could say something.

Ray Why? So you could misinterpret it. Grind it down, round it off. Look, Phoebe asked me to come. I put my work on a laptop. Here I am. And she really thinks my model can –

Nigel I know what Phoebe thinks.

Beat. Ray gets the message.

Ray Do you, now . . .?

Nigel takes Phoebe's glass and drains it. He hands it back to Ray, fired up now.

Nigel Shall I tell you what's gonna happen at this conference? So you're not hanging on in suspense?

Ray You know what's gonna happen?

Nigel Yeah.

Ray You sure?

Nigel I write for the *Guardian*, of course I'm sure. Rich nations have done the bulk of the polluting, poor nations will feel the sharp edge of the problem, but China wants to pull a quarter of a billion people out of poverty and who the hell are we to stop them. They want what we've got and you can't blame them for it. It's Ray, isn't it?

Ray Yes.

Nigel Your security pass says Raymondo.

Ray Probably Phoebe's little joke.

Nigel I don't get it. Still, this all comes down to history, Raymondo. Fault lines, who hates who. Who distrusts who. If we could wipe everyone's memory – get a bunch of seventeen-years-olds in a room, we could fix the problem in forty minutes. History's the problem . . . That's what'll fuck us in the end.

Told you I was clever. Show me your laptop.

Ray I'm freezing to death. Nice to meet you, Nigel.

He turns to head back inside. Nigel takes out another cigarette.

Nigel Whatever you do, don't follow her around like a puppy. She won't like that. I should know.

The music booms, Ray and Nigel melt away. Outside the conference centre protesters chant and march.

FIFTEEN

The Arctic. Harry picks up a guillemot. He measures its wing span.

Harry To kill the Nemean lion, the Lernean hydra and the Stymphalian birds. To capture alive the Erymanthian boar, the Cretan bull and the Ceryneian stag. How am I doing so far?

Harold Six.

Harry turns back to his bird.

Harry 141.

Harold writes it down. Harry puts the wriggling, jiggling bird inside an orange weighing bag.

The secret is to divide them into units. Those Heracles had to kill, those he had to capture alive, now those he had to steal. He had to steal the horses of Diomedes, the girdle of Hippolyta and the apples of Hesperides. My favourite of his twelve tasks because –

Harold It involved Atlas.

Harry Mum loved Atlas. 236. Did you get that?

Harold writes it down.

Harold Yes.

Harry lets the bird go, he moves on. Harold watches him. They move in silence for a moment.

Do you think they're talking to each other?

Harry I think they're communicating.

Harold What do you think they're saying?

Harry laughs.

Harry At a guess? 'Fuck off. This is my spot. Where's the fish? Fuck off. This is my spot. Where's the fish?' And then they might say: 'Fuck off. This is my spot. Where's the fish?'

Harold is laughing.

Harold Don't accuse me of anthropomorphism.

Harry Oh, I'm accusing you of something with considerably less – keep still.

Harry has seen something.

Harold What?

Harry Stay perfectly still.

A polar bear walks onstage. Harold turns and glimpses it and then turns rigidly back to his spot. Both men are petrified.

Keep your voice slow and steady. Don't look in its eyes.

Harold I don't want to look in its eyes.

Harry Stand your ground and try and look as large as possible.

Harold Large as . . .?

Harry OK, after three we're going to raise our hands slowly in the air.

Harold Raise our hands?

Harry One – two – three.

They raise their hands.

Even if it charges you. You stay like that. It's probably bluffing. Don't show fear. Don't show vulnerability.

Harold But I am vulnerable. It could kill me extremely easily.

Harry It doesn't know that.

He thinks.

If he attacks me, get on the radio. Get Mac here.

Harold The Mac that never answers?

Harry That's the one.

Harry thinks how to distract Harold.

The final three – the final three – Heracles' final three tasks. They're not ones you can fit in the kill, capture, steal categories. They're to – clean the Augean stables, to herd the cattle of Geryon and to fetch Cerberus from the underworld.

Harold Herding cattle? That's heroic?

Pause. Harry finds this difficult.

Harry You know to some – I'm a – hero?

Harold Is that right?

Harry Al Gore thinks I'm a hero. Told me.

Harold And does Al Gore get to decide?

Harry laughs a staccato laugh. The polar bear turns in their direction. Harold notices.

Careful.

The polar bear slowly moves towards them.

Harry He certainly thinks so.

The polar bear sniffs Harold's leg. Harold stiffens.

Harold A bear is sniffing my leg, Harry the hero.

Harry Concentrate on me. Concentrate on me, Cambridge boy. He thinks I'm a hero because of my data. My thirty years of data. Because guillemots are Arctic birds whose breeding is responsive to snow-melt, my statistics on their patterns shows what change in Arctic temperatures is doing – the guillemots are natural, real-world evidence that the Arctic summer is arriving earlier.

Harold This isn't distracting me, Harry. Tell me about your sex life.

Harry Every decade their summer has arrived on average five days earlier. That's important.

The polar bear starts moving on.

Harold Is it moving . . .? Is it leaving me? Is it leaving me?

Harry Birds that barely have anything to do with humankind reflecting global warming. That's why I'm a – hero.

Suddenly there is a burst of movement – the polar bear attacks the birds. And then gallops off with a bird in its teeth.

There is a pause that seems to last for ever. Then Harold slowly lowers his arms. Harry keeps his in the air. His eyes on the growing pool of blood the bear left behind.

Harold Harry. It's over. He's gone. He's gone.

Pause.

Harry The bird it took – it left fledglings . . .

Harold Oh . . . Will they – be – OK?

Harry They're going to need a new mother and they're not going to find one.

Harold Shall we pick them up?

Harry The shock will probably kill them.

Harold And if we leave them?

Harry Then they'll definitely die.

Harold thinks and then thinks again and then bends and picks up a fledgling. He holds it in his hands for just a moment.

He says nothing.

The bird dies.

Told you.

Harold Yes.

Pause.

Harry The thing my figures also show is why the guillemots are dying. The Arctic pack-ice was seven miles offshore when I arrived on this island. It's now two hundred and fifty miles. This means cod shortages – which means the birds can't eat. Every year the population of my guillemots declines by fifteen. And it means pack-ice predators like polar bears are being brought on to the island. The bears shouldn't be here.

Pause.

Harry Barrow is the warmest it's been in four hundred years of temperature reading. The permafrost core of this very island is melting. There are turtles on Kodiak Island. There are birds starving on St Lawrence. There are snowmobiles falling through the ice in Nenana. In Canada's Northwest Territories, Inuit Eskimos saw their first robin last summer. There is no word in Inuit for 'robin'.

Harry We'll leave the other one, yeah? Let nature do its worst to the other one.

Harold Yes.

Pause. Harold reaches out to touch Harry. But doesn't.

Harry Do you know what Heracles did after he'd finished his twelve tasks?

Harold I know as much about Heracles as you do.

Harry He became one of the Argonauts searching for the Golden Fleece. Then he became slave to someone for a while. Then he rescued Prometheus. Then he killed a sea monster sent by Poseidon. He never stopped. Do you know why? Because it never felt like enough.

A truly mournful pause.
Then Harold lifts the dead bird – and it takes off and flies away. And they turn and watch it go together.

> *Then Harold falls through a trap in the floor.*
> *And Harry is alone.*
> *He's really truly utterly alone.*

I'm really tired.

SIXTEEN

Ray and Phoebe lie in bed together under the covers,
their eyes glued to a laptop. On a large screen behind
them is Ray's model. It shows an image of the earth and
the heat-scorched areas of mainland Europe and Africa.
It's beautiful but horrific. Phoebe stares at it. Ray
watches her.

Ray Tell me.

Phoebe What?

Ray What you're thinking?

Phoebe I'm thinking about bringing kids into all this . . .

Ray It's a first date, Phoebe. Steady on.

He smiles lamely but she looks at him, unamused.

Phoebe Don't be a dick. You know exactly what I mean.
You built this, you must feel it too.

Ray I should . . . but . . . It's a hard urge to fight.

Phoebe Really? Not for me. Not looking at this.

He closes the laptop and the screen behind them falls
dark. Phoebe's BlackBerry beeps from the end of the
bed but she doesn't move. On the dark screen behind
her the text message appears: TURN ON THE TV!

Ray It's a model. It's just a model.

Phoebe It's your career.

Ray I don't have the answers, OK? I can't know the scale of the problem.

Phoebe But this shows you . . .

Ray A projection. I keep telling you, it's a prototype. We don't even know if the carbon is going to remain in the atmosphere or not. Harm us or not. Or whether nature will have responses we can't even imagine now – trees may start to double their rate of growth so that they can absorb more carbon dioxide.

Phoebe Then what happens?

Ray I don't know.

Phoebe Why not? I thought science could do anything, right?

Phoebe stares forward for a moment before leaning her head on Ray's shoulder. He slips his arm round her and kisses the top of her head. Silence.

The BlackBerry beeps again. The message on the screen reads: SHIT IS HITTING THE FAN DOWN HERE. OBAMA SAYS WE'RE CLOSE TO A DEAL. ON WHAT PLANET?

Silence. It beeps again: FORREST GUMP JUST ASKED FOR YOU. ARE YOU SHAGGING?! *Phoebe reaches casually for the phone but Ray stops her.*

I think I have to get it . . . Something might be happening down there.

Ray It's the middle of the night.

Phoebe The final plenary is still in session.

Ray It's over though, right?

Phoebe Ed will still be there. To the bitter end. He's a machine.

Ray Do you fancy him?

Phoebe No. I've tried . . .

> *They sit in silence for a moment.*
> *Phoebe looks uneasy. She hesitates.*

I'm sorry. For bringing you all this way. You're probably not going to get to talk to anyone now.

Ray Right.

Phoebe I could take the laptop. Try and get it in front of Ed –

Ray It's all right. Most of the facts are known.

Phoebe Not the complete picture.

Ray I'm telling you, there'll never be a complete picture.

Phoebe All your work –

Ray I came for you. I mean . . . (*Beat. Embarrassed.*) Not just for you. But after you visited. The lab . . .

Phoebe What?

Ray I live my life a hundred years in the future. I can't do that for ever. I thought if we could show someone maybe it would be a cut-off point. I think I've been looking for a cut-off point.

> *She pulls away from him slightly.*

Phoebe This is because of . . .? You know, what you've seen, isn't it? The process or whatever. Up close. Don't get disheartened by all this . . .

Ray It's hard not to.

Phoebe But what you do and what you'll go on to do –

Ray I'd rather work in a garden centre. Honestly. I started at the Royal Botanic Gardens, wrote books for them on species. Did a PhD in Maths. Fell in love with modelling, but you can fall out of love just as easily, right?

Phoebe I don't believe you.

Ray Don't be angry.

Phoebe I thought you were one of us. I thought you were a believer.

Ray It's not a religion, Phoebe.

Phoebe Of course it is. Against insurmountable odds, you know, you can't buckle. Something good can still happen here. We need you.

Ray I want a family. I've given ten years of my life to this. Three years to this one model alone. I think that's enough.

Phoebe Not until something changes it isn't. Make a noise, Ray. Tell people what you know. What you've shown me.

Ray That's your job, not mine, and you're failing at it –

Phoebe (*slowly absorbing this, stung*) I could hang off a fucking oil rig, screaming my lungs out. I could be that person. So easily. But this, here, this is how you change things.

Ray You hope.

Phoebe Right now there's a room downstairs. One room and there's no other place, no other room where anything more important is happening.

Ray Then why are you here, with me?

Silence.

What are your plans?

Phoebe What do you mean?

Ray I'd like to see you again. Back home . . .

She is thinking about this for a moment when her BlackBerry beeps again: TURN ON THE FUCKING TV! *She checks her phone and a moment later she suddenly bolts out of bed, naked. She runs around for a moment and Ray watches her.*

What?

Phoebe The remote. Where's the fucking remote . . .?

She throws her clothes about as Ray gets out of bed, also naked, and helps her look. He finds it under his heaped trousers. She snatches the remote from him and turns on the TV. They both stare into the corner at an unseen screen. Behind them on the big screen the footage from the Copenhagen plenary is broadcast. The Sudanese delegate is speaking. Phoebe listens, transfixed.

Ray Who is that?

Phoebe Lumumba. Sudanese delegate. He's the G77 spokesman, the developing nations.

Ray Looks angry.

Phoebe Shhh!

They stand naked and listen. Lumumba slowly speaks and likens 'L9' to the Holocaust, to a suicide pact. Phoebe shakes her head, distraught.

Phoebe That's it . . .

Ray What happened?

Phoebe Didn't you hear him? He just compared the Copenhagen treaty to the Holocaust.

Ray And is he right?

She stares at him. On the screen, Lumumba finishes.
We see Ed Miliband appear and start to speak. Other
delegates watch and listen.

Phoebe I've got to get down there.

Ray What's the point?

Phoebe Maybe we can do something, still. People need
us, Ray. Politics and science.

Ray Come home. With me . . .

She's dressed now. She stares at him, torn.

They don't want a solution. There's too much to lose if
they solve this. Come home . . .

She looks at him and leaves. He sits back on the bed
and turns off the television. Darkness.

SEVENTEEN

It begins to rain. Jeremy Oppenheim, Michael Jacobs
and Joanna Depledge appear.

Oppenheim It absolutely had to happen in the way that
it did.

Depledge Jeremy Oppenheim, Senior Adviser on Global
Sustainabilty and Climate. This is Michael Jacobs. He
was Gordon Brown's Special Adviser at Copenhagen.

Jacobs By the last day we were trying to salvage a deal
among the leaders. It was in a room that could
comfortably seat thirty. There must have been a hundred
and thirty in there – aides, ministers, security. After
about two hours Obama walks in, accompanied by his
bodyguards, straight off Airforce One. Obama takes the

US seat from Hillary Clinton, who comes and squeezes on to the same chair I'm sitting on. It was a surreal sight – the American President, jacket off, negotiating with a middle-ranking Chinese official, because the Chinese premier had chosen to remain in his hotel room.

Depledge Some people blame China. But I think they moved a hell of a lot more historically at Copenhagen than the US did.

Oppenheim We walked in there attempting not just to do a deal in one arena like energy, but something that spanned energy, land use, technology and global finance. All at once. With the unanimity of two hundred countries.

Jacobs Eventually Obama went to meet the Chinese leader face to face. When he got there he found himself confronted not just by Premier Wen Ji-Bao, but by the leaders of India, Brazil and South Africa – the four major emerging nations. They told him that they would agree to the deal, but only on their own terms. And you could sense then, that in that room, a new world order was being born.

Depledge People think that climate change negotiations are about finding the best solution to climate change. They're not. No one is sitting there saying, 'Right, how can we tackle this problem?' It's not like that. Seventy per cent of it is procedural wrangling.

Jacobs After that meeting the thirty leaders finalised the draft. Now it had to be to be agreed by the hundred and sixty nations not in the room. But President Obama, anxious to get home before freezing weather closed the airport in Washington, instead called a press conference and announced that the deal had been done. Well, you can imagine. It was a disaster. The rest of the world was outraged.

Depledge The tiniest of details can ruin something this delicate. A frozen airport . . .

Oppenheim We had walked to the edge of learning what it would mean to live in a more collaborative world – then we walked away from it. The forces that divide us and the forces that lead us to protect our own small piece of the puzzle – we had allowed those to utterly dominate the forces that should unite us.

Depledge A year later the wheels started turning again. In Cancun, Mexico. Another conference, only not so big. No fanfares and no world leaders either, thank God. But some progress. Little by little. South Africa will follow in 2011. No one pretends this system is perfect, but it's the only one we've got.

Alamir and Seydou appear in the rain. They all slowly exit and we hear recordings of 911 calls from disaster zones.

EIGHTEEN

The ocean. Lisa, in a wetsuit, appears. She talks to Paula on Skype.

Lisa Hello, Mum.

Paula Lisa.

Lisa I'm missing you.

Paula You look like someone off *Blue Peter*.

Lisa I'm learning to dive.

Paula Well, fantastic.
What are you doing that for?

Lisa We might be going out to Papua New Guinea.

I'm hoping we won't need to but –
There's a gas pipeline planned out there and
We might . . . go to try and stop it.

Paula Why's the gas pipeline your problem, Lisa?

Lisa Mum, it's everybody's problem.

Paula Why specifically yours? What about the Papua
New Guineans? Don't they have anybody qualified to
sort it out? Why does my daughter have to do it?

Lisa (*sighs*) Why can't you support me, Mum?

Paula Where's your Dave then?

Lisa Dav. He's with . . . what's her name.

Paula Who's what's her name?

Lisa Celia.
She's helping us.

Paula Lisa.
People who have fervour, who have clear ideas,
I can see why they're attractive when you're lost.
We don't have a lot of fervour nowadays / and –

Lisa Do you think I'm lost?

Paula I think you're searching for the right direction.
I'm not sure you've found it yet.

Lisa I love him, Mum.

Paula Then he's very lucky, isn't he?
I hope he sees it.

Dav and Celia appear. They are passionately arguing.

Dav And I don't believe the lies that capitalism tells
about choice and freedom. It's bullshit.

Celia How can freedom be bullshit?

Dav We're in an iron cage of consumerism.

Celia Our power as consumers has given us our freedom. Economic growth emancipated us.

Dav It's a fucking monster. The corporations have more power than the people we've elected. Government is totally subservient to economic interest.

Celia Democracy you mean. You think democracy's subservient.

Dav I think that capital is running Capitol Hill.

Celia You think the market is the problem?
  I can tell you now, it's the market that will fix this.

Dav / Oh for fuck's sake, that's deluded.

Celia Government needs to put a price on carbon now. A high price. / And provide incentives for developing clean energies.

Dav You're still talking about growth and not sustainability.

Celia Then the market – of its own volition / will swing away from fossil fuels.

Dav There won't be an incentive. Because big oil is holding government to ransom.

Celia The market needs to put a price on the world's resources – forests, for example –

Lisa / You're making me die.

Celia Making our natural resources more viable to keep than to destroy –

Lisa / I'm dying, Celia.

Celia With things like cap-and-trade and carbon offsets.

Lisa / Cap-and-trade? Carbon offsets?

Celia Industry will regulate itself and our emissions automatically will start to fall.

Dav That's a billion, billion-dollar stitch-up. That is paying to pollute. That's like selling speeding permits, saying, 'Well, we don't approve of all the speeding going on and we wish it wasn't happening, but we can't stop it so we'll make some money / from it –'

Celia It's *cap*-and-trade. Cap. They put a limit on it.

Lisa 'So we're going to give out speeding permits and if you're a tosspot in a BMW and you're using all your permits up, I'll sell you one of mine because I'm just a wanker with a small electric car.'

Celia OK, if the market can't expand and if contraction spells disaster – because it always has – what's the solution?

Dav Well, Celia, you'll have to give me time on that because I'm just a twenty-six-year-old from Swansea and as yet I haven't managed to work out our new financial order.

Celia Wait –
  Hold still.

Dav What?

Celia Eyelash.

She picks an eyelash off his cheek.

Make a wish, it's lucky.

Dav is quite arrested by the sweetness of this gesture. He blows the eyelash away. He looks at Celia, surprised.

Lisa Why don't you kiss each other?

They have both forgotten that Lisa is there.

Seriously, you know you want to –

Dav Lisa,
Don't embarrass us.

Pause.

Celia Excuse me.

Celia dives backwards off the side of the boat and into the sea.

Lisa Are you shagging her?

Dav We couldn't help it.
It just happened.

Lisa But you don't agree with anything she says.

Dav I know.
But the way she argues –

Lisa Awwwoooww . . .

Dav I'm sorry.

Lisa Awwwoooww . . .

Dav Lisa –
You're –

Lisa I'm going home.

Dav Don't give up.

Lisa I'm not giving up.
How dare you think that I'd give up because of you.
I'm going home to get a job
With Greenpeace.

Dav Greenpeace? Don't sell out,
Lisa.

Lisa Someone will appreciate my skills.

And they leave in opposite directions.

NINETEEN

Adeel appears, centre stage, with his box.

Adeel You know another thing about human beings?
Despite everything, we believe, Mum and me, we believe
we're all . . . valuable. You know? And I don't mean
   I mean I'm trying not to think like
   how my value is
   dependent on what amount of money it says inside
this box?
   Because it can't be true. That like
   how much you're worth is just down to that.
   One p.
Two hundred and fifty thousand pounds. Some kind of
random distribution of numbers. Money. It can't just be
about that. Can it? We're all
   important. I think. Because I do believe we're all –
   All human beings are fundamentally good. Inside. And
you know how I know? Because when you watch this
show –
   One thing remains true. Whoever is playing, your
natural human instinct is to want that person to win.
You hear their dreams. Their problems. And whoever
they are and wherever they come from –
   You hope
   You have hope for their future, yeah?

He goes to open his box.

She said don't end up with a one-box game. You can't
stake your whole future on just
   one

79

solution. But here I am. Down to the last piece of toilet roll. Yet again. And you can judge me if you want, yeah? But if you do . . .

I dunno. If you do . . .

All I can do is I just got to believe there's still hope. I got to believe I can still win. Yeah? Because it's like I said, yeah. Probability

means nothing

when you only get one chance. I can still

win. It might be OK. And I know you want that. I know you still want me to win. Don't you?

He tears off the tag. He puts his hands on the side.

Don't you?

He opens it. Light shines out of the box. There is a crash and he races offstage.

TWENTY

A restaurant appears. Ray waits, but only for a moment. A young Waiter brings Phoebe over and gestures to the table. Ray stands and they awkwardly kiss one another on both cheeks. She sits and the Waiter pushes in the chair and steps away. She still has her handbag on her lap. Ray smiles at her.

Ray Good choice, bad choice?

Phoebe (*looks around*) It's all right. But you know me, I normally hate the South Bank, there's always some prick on a unicycle. You look nice.

Ray Thank you. You look –

Phoebe I've put on weight. (*She pulls her bag close to hide her tummy.*)

Ray I don't think –

Phoebe It's campaign food. It's eating crap at all hours.

Ray You look great.

Phoebe I've put on a stone.

Ray Fuck?! Really . . . Where?

Phoebe All over. Evenly distributed.

Ray I can't tell.

Phoebe Thank you, Ray.

Phoebe takes her bag from her lap. She fishes around for her new iPhone before putting it on the table and the bag at her feet. Phoebe picks up her menu. Ray watches her.

I never really look at a menu, I just sort of glaze over. Pick for me?

Ray nods and she shuts the menu. They look at each other for a moment. Her iPhone beeps and she reaches for it, but without hesitation Ray picks it up, stands and throws it with all his might to the back of the restaurant. We don't see it land. He sits down again and she looks at him.

Better?

Ray Yes.

Phoebe You fucking child . . . It'll find its way back to me.

Ray Is there an app for that?

She looks angry, on the front foot now.

Phoebe What do you want?

Ray To see you. In the flesh.

Phoebe Here I am.

Ray How's Red Ed?

Phoebe Powerful-ish.

Ray I keep seeing you in the paper. In the corner of photographs. He's striding into buildings and you're holding things, striding alongside him. I only ever see half of you.

Phoebe I told you I'd put on weight.

Ray You look so very determined. Arrow straight.

Phoebe Truth be told I'm trying not to trip over in front of the *Daily Mail*.

Ray Maybe you should. Ed could pick you up, he'd look heroic.

Phoebe I'll bring it up at morning briefing, see if it flies.

The waiter arrives with a tray and fizzy water. He pours the water and then takes the iPhone from the tray and lays it down in front of Phoebe.

Waiter This slipped out of sir's hand.

Phoebe Thank you.

Waiter My boss says if he does that again he'll call the police.
Are you ready to order?

Ray Sea bass. Twice.

Phoebe Hang on. Where's it from? Because if it's Chilean I don't want it, I'm sorry. If it's Chilean sea bass I'll have a Caesar salad instead.

Ray watches her and smiles.

Ray Same.

The Waiter takes the menus and withdraws. Phoebe checks her iPhone and puts it back down in front of her. She looks at Ray.

Phoebe So. Hit me . . . What's so important?

Ray (*hesitating*) I need a little more small talk first. One more go around.

She seems surprised at his unease. She adjusts but still has an edge to her.

I got a new job. Classroom assistant.

Phoebe (*mixed*) That's brilliant.

Ray How's the five-year plan?

Phoebe It's early days. We're finding our feet. Refining the message.

Ray And after that?

Phoebe After that we're gonna win the next fucking election . . .

Ray And then what? Another five-year plan?

Phoebe What's the point of all this if it isn't to win? You've got to win in order to do something. It's a long game. We have to play it that way.

Ray We?

Phoebe Everyone who's engaged in it. Who's put their life on hold. We're not all quitters, Ray.

Ray Copenhagen.

Silence.

Phoebe I still believe in everything we tried to do there. It isn't dead.

Ray But it isn't what you do now. Not day to day.

Phoebe It's someone else's brief.

Ray It's all a bit too 2009, isn't it . . . ?

Silence.

Phoebe Your email –

Silence.

Ray Look. Listen to me. This is gonna be tricky. But I'm going to . . .
This is going to change everything between us.

His face changes. She suddenly leans forward and takes his hand.

Phoebe Hey . . . What is it? It's OK . . . You can tell me.

Ray I'm having our baby.

She looks at him for a long time. Slowly, by degrees she looks more and more angry. She withdraws her hand from his and crosses her arms. He looks at her.

Phoebe I came across town for this.

Ray I've had tests.

Phoebe You've had . . .

She starts laughing, she can't help herself. She laughs long and hard and then abruptly she stops. She takes a sip of water and picks up her iPhone and stands.

Don't call me, or text me or whatever.

She stands. He looks at her.

Ray It isn't in my body. I don't have a womb so obviously I can't carry it inside me.

Phoebe You don't have a womb? Was that a shock to you . . . ?

Ray When we slept together –

84

Phoebe A year ago.

Ray It takes longer for a man.

Phoebe Aren't you embarrassed? This is . . . desperate.

Ray Endocytosis. The process by which cells absorb foreign molecules. I absorb a few of your cells into my body during intercourse. It happens all the time. Two bodies can't penetrate one another and not leave a trace behind. An imprint. It would come to nothing unless you found a way to extract what was left behind. The DNA sample of you, left in my body. If it can be identified and extracted then the principle of IVF can be applied to it. A test tube. (*Beat.*) My body incubated cells from your body and then they were extracted and now there's a life. Science can do anything . . .

She stares at him, speechless. He has a sip of water and looks down at his hands. She takes a seat and continues to stare.

Phoebe I . . . How long?

Ray (*looks up at her slowly and then smiles*) Your face!

Phoebe You bastard!

Ray You gullible cow. Still!

Phoebe You total shit. Worse-case scenario . . .

Ray Our little game. I thought you'd remember.

He's laughing now and after a moment she's laughing too.

Phoebe What?

Ray Whatever is gonna happen if you get back into government?

She shakes her head and her laughter stops.

Phoebe Is that it? Is that why I came? So you could laugh at me?

Ray I miss it.

Silence. He leans across towards her.

Are you –?

Phoebe Am I?

Ray Is there anyone?

Phoebe When would there be anyone? When could there possibly be anyone for me? At 12.45 at night for ten minutes, while I get undressed, take my make-up off. Leave reminder messages for myself, on my own voicemail. Fancy that? Sound sexy to you?

Ray I'd do it.

Phoebe I bet.

Ray I would. I still fancy the pants off you.

Phoebe Thanks.

Ray I love you . . .

She closes her eyes.

Let's have a family.

Phoebe Out of your tummy?

Ray Out of yours. Or we adopt.

Phoebe (*quietly, shaking her head*) Ray . . .

Ray I'd have a meal on the table every night. I'd research solar panels. Change the bulbs. Recycle. I'd raise our kids while you work yourself to death.

Phoebe Kids?

Ray We shouldn't be the ones who don't have them.

Phoebe Then who should?

Ray I don't know.

Silence. The Waiter brings over their food and sets it down. Ray sits back while the Waiter lays a napkin on his lap. He does the same for Phoebe.

Waiter It's locally sourced. Whitstable. That all right for you?

Phoebe That's fine, thank you.

Waiter Parmesan?

Ray With fish . . . ?

The Waiter shrugs and walks away. Phoebe looks at Ray and picks up her fork. She starts to eat. He starts to eat. Silence. She is thinking, wrestling with herself. He looks up and spots her watching him.

What?

Phoebe OK . . .

They look at each other. Her iPhone beeps. They both stare at it. Darkness.

TWENTY-ONE

The Arctic. Night. Lisa abseils down. She's underneath an oil rig.

Lisa We've held up the drilling for two days now.

Al Why, Lisa? I mean, it's all very David and Goliath, but you know they're going to get you down, love, and then they're going to prosecute you. And you might make a paragraph on the news but they're still going to open up that well and drill.

Lisa Dad . . . it's deepwater drilling in the Arctic Circle. We've crossed a threshold. And it must be marked. I know two days is just a blip but . . . that's what it is, a

pause, a breath, where we can look at it. Bear witness,
my boss says – where we can really think, is this the
future that we want?

Paula Are you warm enough, my love?

Lisa I'm OK, Mumz.
  The colours in the dark are beautiful.
  And I wish you understood why I am here.

Paula He wants to say he's proud of you.

Lisa Are you?

Al You be careful up there.

Lisa I've prob'ly gone a bit light-headed cos it's cold. But
what I'm thinking is, we're coming to a massive change,
a transformation. It frightens me, but it inspires me too.
I don't know what to do with it. It's so big I can't fit it
in my head. All of us, we've got to choose what that
transformation is.

Paula You've been a gift to us.

Al Exceptional –

Lisa I've never ever felt so tiny and so ordinary.

She abseils down and off as Freya and Sarah appear.

Freya She says
  I make her feel guilty about everything. Her jeans. Her
shoes. What she drinks. Holidays. Driving. She said the
other day she caught herself apologising
  to a piece of broccoli
  for not eating it. She says
  she just wants to go back to how things were. Before
all this was a problem. When it was all just hairsprays
and keeping the fridge door shut. She says
  other people don't think like this. And I say that's the
whole problem. And she says: but why does it have to be
us? She says –

One time she said I'm like a hamster on a wheel
running
running
thinking I'm getting somewhere. There's nothing we
can do, she says. But it's like I always say to her:
You didn't see it.
Once you've seen it
you can't close your eyes
you have to stand. You have to fight. There's no going
back.

We hear the creak of a huge wall of ice. Behind them
it slowly collapses with a monumental crash.

Sarah She makes me feel guilty about everything. My
shoes. A cup of coffee. She thinks I don't believe it, but
I do. She's seen the ice. I do believe. But at the same
time . . .
It's not like I don't ever watch the news. I see the fires.
The floods. But two minutes later it's all about the
recession. Or some – election. On Monday they say this
could be the end of the world! –
Then on Tuesday they make me feel bad for not
having a pension.
They say we're all going to die. Then there's an ad
break full of happy songs and adverts for airlines.
They say we're on the brink of an environmental
catastrophe of global proportions!
Act now! And sometimes when I'm feeling brave I say
OK then. What do you want me to do?
And they tell me to rinse and recycle a milk bottle.
Change a fucking lightbulb? How do you want me to
feel? You're telling me to fight. But it's like saying there's
an army coming
with guns and bombs and cannons
and all I've got
is this rubber knife.

They move off as we fade into the Arctic.

TWENTY-TWO

Harry sits on the stage. The snow is falling around him. The sun is low in the sky.
   Harold emerges. He has a morning face.

Harry This is the time I like best . . .

   Harold thinks, focuses and speaks with sleep in his voice.

Harold The time when you're really tired, it's freezing and you just want to crawl back into your sleeping bag and die?

Harry The time when the sun hasn't set or risen but snow petrels still sing the dawn chorus.

Harold The time when the madness of this place is clearest. That makes sense.

   Harry looks at Harold and smiles.

Harry This place isn't mad.

Harold They say that the best indicator of madness isn't looking for hairs on the palm of your hand. It's shaving your palm to be rid of them.

   Harry thinks.

Harry You'll go today.

Harold Will I?

Harry Yes.

Harold Right.

   This moment is important. Both men know it.

Harry Any last words?

   Harold thinks.

Harold This is the last of earth. I am content. John Quincy Adams.

Harry Ha! I like that.

Harold Friends, applaud. The comedy has finished. Ludwig Van Beethoven.

Harry Either that wallpaper goes, or I do. Oscar Wilde.

Harold I'm bored with it all. Winston Churchill.

Harry I am not the least afraid to die. Charles Darwin.

Harold That is –

Harry I am just going outside and I may be some time. Captain Lawrence 'Titus' Oates.

Harold I know you have come to kill me. Shoot, coward, I am only a man. Che Guevara.

Harry Go on, get out. Last words are for fools that have not said enough. Karl Marx.

Pause. And then another pause. A chair appears and Harold moves towards it.

What if I . . . wasn't . . . didn't . . . What if I wasn't enough?

The Cambridge scene fades back into view. Robert is speaking.

Robert Harold, I don't mean to stop you mid-flow, but is your father one of those – encyclopedia salesmen? Because I assure you one thing I don't need is the *Britannica* definition of geography.

Harold sits on the chair.
The company have formed in a line behind the scene. A line that moves slowly forward as the scene progresses.

Harry No. My father was not a salesman.

Harold My father's in post offices, sir. He runs a post office in Walthamstow.

Robert I'll make this easy. You applied for Geography because you thought you'd get in. You're a working-class boy on the make, part of me admires that. Geography is a comparatively new subject for Cambridge – well, 1888, ergo a comparatively easy subject to crack. Though I'd tell you now, you'd have been better applying for Theology, as . . .

Harold (*interrupts*) Did you read about the oil spill? Sir? The *Torrey Canyon* oil spill?

Robert You are asking me whether I've read? Again. Prizes for novelty. Intimidate the interviewer.

Harold No, I . . .

Robert Go right ahead. I think it's something most of us have heard about it – even if our parents don't run post offices. Talk to me like I haven't heard about it . . .

Harry The last day of every season is identical. I check the sky – to see whether the helicopter can land – and if it looks positive and I've had no radio signals to contradict, I'll drink a cup of hot chocolate whilst smoking the one cigarette I bring to the island with me. I smoke to the butt, till it's dead. Used to be a large smoker. I was a nervous teenager. And we didn't really know better then.

And then I walk due east on a final four-mile tour of my terrain. Through my birds. My – birds.

Harold Initially they used detergents to counteract the oil in *Torrey Canyon*. Then they used foam booms to try and contain it – that didn't work either. Then they used bombers – Buccaneer bombers to sink the tanker and its deadly contents – forty-two bombs dropped off the coast of Cornwall. Then they tried to use this substance called napalm to burn off the slick. Everything failed. One hundred and twenty miles of coastland afflicted. Fifteen thousand birds killed.

Robert These are just facts. Everyone knows – your namesake – Harold – Wilson has made a balls-up of it.

Harold Do you know the story of Heracles?

Robert Greek myth now – You do hop about . . .

Harold My mum had this book of Greek myths. She'd read them to me. There are two things people never remember about him – the first is why he had to do his twelve tasks –

Robert Hera bewitched him into killing his own children. The tasks were penance.

Harold OK. So – some people know –

Robert (*grins*) You do understand that this place is an educated place for educated people?

Harold The second thing people seem to always not know – is that Heracles chose his life. Do you know that bit, sir?

Robert thinks and then smiles.

Robert You know, I don't. Go on.

Harold Prodicus, sir – 'The Choice of Heracles'.
Heracles was sent by his foster father to tend cattle on a mountain. There he was met by two nymphs – virtue and vice. Though vice is sometimes known as pleasure. Which I think is a better name because vice didn't offer sin – vice simply offered doing the easy things which would make him happy. But virtue – virtue offered – seeing the world as it is.

Robert Now you're sounding like a philosopher, Harold. This is a Geography interview.

Harry The last day of season. I check – see whether the helicopter can – and if it looks, I'll drink a cup of hot chocolate whilst smoking till it's dead. I was a nervous teenager. And we didn't really know better then. And then I walk due east on a final four-mile tour of my terrain. Through my birds. My – birds.

Harold He chose virtue. He'd kill his kids. He'd later kill his best friend. He'd live a life defined by pain and slavery to others' whims. But he saw the world as it was. And I think – um . . . I go birdwatching every weekend – sometimes with my friend in Epping Forest. Other times on Barn Hill in Wembley on my own. We found an American robin the other day. I don't know how it got there. But it shouldn't have been there. Whatever bought it there was something we did. Whatever happens to the Cornish coast now is something we've done. Something which will have changed seabird stocks on the southern coast for ever. Geography – for me – is about habitat – how we fit in the world, how the world fits us.

Pause. Robert smiles.

It's about seeing the world as it is, not how you want the world to be. That's exciting. Because the world is changing, sir. And I'm excited by watching that change.

Harry The last day. Sky – see whether – and if looks and no . . . I'll drink. Dead. Dead. Used to be. I was. And we didn't really know. And then I walk on a – final. Through – my birds. / My – birds.

Harry joins the rest of the company in a line across the stage.

Robert You intrigue me. Harold. I think you have possibilities. You're the sort of boy who could grow up to be William Beveridge or – Guido Fawkes . . .

Harold Thank you, sir.

Harold gets up to leave.

Robert The way I remember you, all – you students – is I write a little comment beside each of you – a memory aid. For Leon, who just came in, lovely boy – Scottish glacial mountains – because he talked very interestingly about Scottish glaciers – what do you think I should write for you?

Harold considers this. And turns to look at him.

Harold Walthamstow, sir. You should write Walthamstow, sir.

Robert smiles.

Robert Always interesting what students reply to that one.

Harold I'll send the next one in.

Robert and Harold join the company in a line. The wind grows, and the sound of a helicopter landing. Snow is blown off around the stage and the auditorium. We hear a voice shouting into the wind.

Mac Harry? Harry. Where are you . . .?
Harry? It's Mac. Don't fuck around.
I've got to – I'm burning fuel. I've got to be at Barrow by five. I've thawing samples in the can.
Harry? Harry? Where are you? Harry?
Fuck. Harry? Harry? Harry?

The snow consumes everyone.